you are

you closer to

in His word & stop

hiding, & running from God.

He loves you!

How *to* Turn *your*
Life Arou⮌d

MO BROOKS

Published in collaboration with
Cover and book design: Jose Pepitojr
Developmental editing: Maleah Bell
Copyediting: Shana Murph

For information regarding this book, bulk discounts, or
speaking engagements, please contact Morris Brooks
at info@mobrooks1.com or visit mobrooks1.com

Library of Congress Cataloging-in-Publication Data
Brooks, Morris, 20xx-
180/ Morris Brooks- Non-fiction
p.cm
1. Christian Life 2. Self-help 3. Non Fiction

ISBN-978-0-578-70492-0

Printed in the United States of America

2020—FIRST EDITION
10 9 8 7 6 5 4 3 2 1

I dedicate this book to my wife, Dayon, who has seen me at my best and my worst. She has allowed God to work on me, and I am grateful to have her in my life. Through all my 180s she holds me accountable and brings the best out of me. I love you, my love. Thank you for your love, patience, and support.

Dayon and I enjoying one of the seven natural wonders of the world, the Grand Canyon.

CONTENTS

Foreword ix

Introduction xi

◆ **CHAPTER 01**   Rethink 1

◆ **CHAPTER 02**   Renounce 21

◆ **CHAPTER 03**   Redirect 37

◆ **CHAPTER 04**   Rehearse 53

Final Words 63

Notes 65

FOREWORD

What happens when it seems that your life is spiraling out of control and there is no way to turn it around? You've tried to change on your own, but your effort has yielded no results. Your thinking seems to be heading in the wrong direction. Your values seem to be heading in the wrong direction. Your relationships seem to be heading in the wrong direction. Your health seems to be heading in the wrong direction. Your finances seem to be heading in the wrong direction. What do you do when your life is at the point of no return? Well, you make a decision to change and enlist a qualified helper like Mo Brooks to assist you in making a 180 in your life.

Mo Brooks is a life strategist who majors in life change, and this book serves as a practical resource guide that will enable you to turn your life around in any area. I've known Mo for more than ten years. I am blessed that he is my brother, friend, and the godfather to my daughter. I've had the privilege to witness how he has overcome struggles and obstacles to turn his own life around. He's the poster child for how to make U-turns in your life. I've seen him rally to write an incredible book called Unmasked, while going to school and working full-time. I've seen him turn bad grades into good grades and graduate from Western Michigan University. I've seen him transition from making unwise financial decisions to making well-informed financial decisions. I've seen and heard testimonies of how he has changed lives for the better through his dynamic writing and speaking. Mo is a living example that it is never too late to change your life. His life reminds us that even if your life is headed in the wrong direction, by God's grace, you can turn it around and go in the right direction.

I am elated that you are reading this book, and I know 180 will be mind-blowing and revolutionary to your life. Get ready for your perspective to be expanded, your potential to be realized, and your life's path to be enlightened. Expect to see immediate results in your life when you apply the principles and concepts in this book.

Rev. Ryan Jackson, MBA
Christian Education Director
Mt. Zion Baptist Church
Kalamazoo, Michigan

INTRODUCTION

The sun was beaming with no shade in sight. You could hear people of all ages screaming and talking. Birds were searching for food anywhere they could get it. It seemed that everyone except me was walking in every direction. My heart beat fast, and tears began to well up in my eyes. I just stood there, lost in Cedar Point Amusement Park in Sandusky, Ohio.

When I left the restroom I must have made a wrong turn, because my parents were nowhere in sight. I had a critical decision to make. I could keep walking, knowing that if I had not seen them yet then I probably would not magically bump into them. On the other hand, I could admit I didn't know where I was going, turn around, and try a different direction. I choose option number two.

To my surprise my parents were in the same location waiting for me to arrive and were holding ice-cold water for me. I did a 180-degree turn that day at Cedar Point. That 180-degree turn saved my parents from a lot of emotional stress, such as the worrying that I had been kidnapped or feeling guilty because they lost their son at the park. That 180 saved me from getting into trouble for not following directions in the first place and from the stress of not being where I was supposed to be. Just as I did a 180 in the amusement park that day, you may need to do a 180 in your life.

Think about your life's dreams, goals, and desires. You may want to have a loving and healthy family. You may want financial and personal freedom. You may desire to stand on your own two feet and not have to rely on your parents. You may want to live a debt-free life so you can help others who are in need. These dreams and goals are great; but what happens when you encounter habits, obstacles, and shortcomings along the way? What happens when your life goes in the wrong direction?

I will never forget the numbing and dark times in my life. My life was headed in the wrong direction. It seemed as if I couldn't catch a break. It seemed that nothing went my way. Every decision I made seemed to be the wrong one and produced a horrible outcome. My bad habits were out of control. I couldn't stop smoking, drinking alcohol, or lying; and I blamed my father for my shortcomings. At the time I thought I had good reason. After all, when I was fifteen years old, after years of abuse, my dad tried to kill my mom by stabbing her three times in the chest. I realized that if I wanted to change my life, I must turn around and go the other way, just as I did on that hot day at Cedar Point.

Honestly, *wanting* to turn your life around is not that hard to understand. I think a lot of people know they need to do a 180 and know what they actually need to change. For whatever reason, actually *changing* is extremely difficult. In my first book, *Unmasked*, I shared a lot of my struggles, skeletons in the closet, and flat-out dumb decisions. I shared how I stole a gaming system from my best friend's apartment, even though I had my own. How dumb is that? I also shared how I have unmasked in more than fifty areas in my life, and I provided practical principles for that.

In *180: How to Turn your Life Around*, I will share the process for how I changed my life. I will share with you a practical guide to how you can do a 180 and turn your own life around.

Turning your life around is bigger than you. When you make a turn in the right direction, there is a ripple effect on everyone around you. The people you love most are greatly and positively impacted by your actions. I want to help you be a blessing to your family, friends, and company. In order to make a difference and fulfill your potential, you may need to do a 180.

Some of you have picked up this book because you want to support me. For that, I want to say thank you for your love and encouragement. You may have picked up this book for yourself or for someone else because you know change is needed. I am here to walk you through this great process so you can enjoy your ice-cold water.

◆ HOW TO USE THIS BOOK

This book will help you answer the question of what area of your life is going in the wrong direction. It will also highlight key areas that you may want to consider and evaluate. You can get as detailed as you like. This book also functions as a guideline on how to do a 180. As you read, stop and reflect upon your life, take notes, and apply the beneficial principles. Answer every question with 100 percent honesty.

I tried to keep *180: How to Turn your Life Around* short and sweet, because almost everything within its pages is geared toward application. You have to read the chapters and follow the instructions consistently in order to turn your life around. You can have all the right information; but without the correct application, your information is useless. Application of the right information is the key that unlocks all of your wildest dreams and provides everything you need for your 180.

So, with that, let's get right to it!

RETHINK

"A man who is lost in a forest and knows he is lost may find his way out. A man lost in a forest and does not know he is lost is in greater trouble for that man is deceived."[1] Do not be deceived; if you are lost, be real about it.

Rethinking is the foundation and most important part of the entire 180 process. If you do not rethink often who you are, why you are here, who you love, and what you do, then the rest of this book or any other book will do you no good. You have to be willing to think differently and admit some difficult things. Telling yourself you are wrong is not easy. Who likes to be wrong? I don't. A 180 can happen only if you are honest with yourself and admit that your thinking is all wrong, especially if your entire life is headed in a bad direction.

Recently I felt a certain way about my wife. We were in the process of buying a house, and we had a home inspection. I was able to attend the home inspection, and she was not. After the inspection she asked me to give her all the details because she was worried about the report. When I told her about the inspection, she said, "OK" and called two other people to ask them the same questions I had just answered. They told her the exact same thing I said. I felt that she did not trust me, and I got into my feelings very quickly. As usual, she noticed my countenance and asked me what was wrong. I said nothing the first two times she asked; then I finally broke. I told her how I felt, and her response made me rethink.

She explained how she always look for confirmation with any big decision. She listens to different people whom she trusts concerning the same situation, so she can solidify her thoughts about the decision. She told me that I am a person she trusts to the highest degree. It was not that my wife did not trust me. I needed to understand the way my wife processes in the area of decision-making. I could have stayed in my feelings or I could rethink. I chose to rethink and make some adjustments to my attitude about the entire situation. This may seem to be a small thing to you, but my marriage (an important area of my life) is better because I made the decision to rethink.

So, my thinking was the first thing that I had

to change. I had to come to the realization that my thoughts were wrong. That is hard for a lot of people either because of the way they were raised or they have rehearsed thinking that way for so long it is hard to give up. In the rest of this chapter, I will be focusing on seven things you must rethink if you are going to do a 180 in your life.

◆ RETHINK YOU

Eric Thomas said, "Self-assessment is not always easy. In fact, it is difficult, if not painful, for most people to acknowledge their own weakness. It is what some would refer to as blind spots. Which in this case, is nothing more than an aspect of your life that you are unaware of."[2] The ability to self-assess is the single most important thing for anyone to master.

How sad a commentary when individuals walk around as though they know all the answers, when in actuality they do not have a clue about what is going on. It is embarrassing when people think they are doing great in a certain area and that is really not the case at all. I have actually thought I could sing, but I have never sung in front of others seriously. One day I tried to lead a song for my youth group in church, and they literally volunteered themselves to lead the song because my singing was so terrible. I was embarrassed and was confronted with the naked truth about myself. I could not get mad at the kids for giving me honest feedback.

When someone tells another person that he or she is not as good as the person thinks, sometimes the person receiving the feedback gets upset, accuses the other person of "hating," and ignores the great feedback he or she has received. This is a serious virus that has spread all over the world and it is known as the *inability to self-assess.*

Chances are, if you are human, you've had experience with this virus. I, myself, am very acquainted with this illness, and I can say firsthand that it is painful to see yourself not as good as you thought you were. This 180 will happen only if you do the painful work of truly assessing yourself. Here are the symptoms:

- Gets angry or frustrated when receiving feedback or construtive crtiticsm
- Never seeks out areas of improvement and always seeks praise for a job well done
- Blames others for why he or she did not do his or her best work
- Thinks her or she deserves, more than others, to be doing a particular thing

The cure for this virus is to humble yourself and acknowledge you are not that good, flawless, or profound. If you are not the best in the world at whatever you are trying to accomplish then, you have room for improvement and growth. Until then, put down your pride and say, "I am not perfect, and I have room to grow, improve, and get better." Once you adopt this attitude, nothing can stop you from making that 180 in your life. I promise you this: if you do not cultivate the ability to self-assess, then you will be stuck—always wondering why change is not happening.

So, what are your strengths and weaknesses? Be honest! Below is a list of personal character traits. Put a circle around your strong areas and a box around your weak areas:

POSITIVE CHARACTER TRAITS

Bold   Calm   Cautious   Decisive
Professional Easygoing Efficient
Alert   Empathetic   Focused
Gentle   Forgiving   Generous
Happy   Honest   Humble
Witty   Funny   Unselfish
Loyal   Obedient   Patient
Playful   Adventurous
Persuasive   Private   Spiritual

Now, let's turn those weaknesses into strengths. Character traits can always be strengthened, by the way, no matter how strong or weak. Make sure you only strengthen the traits you absolutely need to make a 180-degree turn in your life.

◆ RETHINK YOUR VALUES

In order to rethink our values we must understand what we currently value. We discover what we currently value by how we spend our time and money. Your family is not one of your top values if you do not spend time with them. When it comes to what you value, the words you speak do not matter; your actions do.

Do not say you value time, while wasting four hours per day scrolling social media feeds. Do not say you value your health, while you refuse to exercise or restrain yourself from eating junk food all the time. Do not say you value your faith in Jesus, while not attending church, reading your Bible, and applying what it says. The reason we need to rethink our values is because the things we consider to be top values are not actually our top values.

What are your real priorities? Where do you spend the most time and money (outside of necessary bills and work requirements)? You cannot just list your values and be done. You have to make your values a priority or they are not values; they are desires. Desires are something you wish you could obtain. Here is where the hard decision comes in. Can you be honest with yourself, even if it hurts?

What are your top five values? Not desires—values. Be honest! This is a no-judgment zone. Circle your top five below:

Cars   Money   Health   Career

Ministry   Sex   Social   Media

Growth   Accomplishments/Awards

Cell Phone   Family   House   Travel

God/Jesus/Holy Spirit   Fun   Friends

Education/Learning   Happiness   Sleep

Race/Ethnicity   Video   Games

Television/Movies   Sports   Smoking

Drinking   Hobbies

◆ RETHINK YOUR LOVE

My definition of *priorities* is this: priorities are the things we do to fulfill our values. Priorities are all about action. That is why I am asking you to rethink your love, because love is about action. Saying you love someone does not mean you do. Whoever or whatever you love will find its way to the top of your priority list. For example, because I value and love my family, eating dinner together every night is a priority. You see, my priority of eating dinner with my family helps to safeguard the thing I say I value and love. Now, more goes into my family, but this is one example. Your priorities will always expose what you really value. The five things you circled in the above activity do not matter if your priorities do not align with those values. Therefore, you must rethink your love.

What are your top five desired values? This list should include the top five values you would pick if we lived in a perfect world. Remember, be totally honest.

1. _____

2 _____

3. _____

4. _____

5. _____

Now, based on those values, what should be your priorities? What should you be doing daily, weekly, and monthly to ensure that what you love prioritized? This list should not be exhaustive. I just want you to get a feel for what I am talking about, so later on you can make as many adjustments as needed. List your priorities below:

1. _____

2 _____

3. _____

4. _____

5. _____

Here is the hard part. It is time to adjust your daily actions so that who or what you love is a reflection of what you reallyalue. Just making this one adjustment is life-changing. Dig deep if you are on the right track already; there are always adjustments we can make in order to improve.

◆ RETHINK YOUR PRINCIPLES

Your principles are what keeps your values intact. Our lives start going in the wrong direction when we are not living out our values or if we have the wrong values altogether. *Principles* are guidelines that you follow to safeguard and prioritize who or what you love, which in turn hold together your values. Principles are the "rules" you follow in order to protect your priorities. You must rethink your principles if you are going to do a 180.

My friend Ryan is always talking about nonnegotiables. Nonnegotiables are principles that are not up for discussion. For example, cheating on my wife (physically or emotionally) is nonnegotiable. It is not an option to consider. It would be wise for you to determine your nonnegotiables.

Let us stick with the family example. I value my family, so my priority is to eat dinner together. When I eat dinner with my family, I talk to my wife with respect. I do not raise my voice, I am concerned about her well-being, and I listen to her. It does not matter how I feel or if I had a bad day. The principles I live by guard me against snapping at my wife or disrespecting her because I had a bad day or a disagreement.

What principles do you live by? I happen to get all of my principles from the Bible. I know people who make up their own rules and live by them. I used to be one of them. I did whatever I felt at the moment. I would live by immoral rules and then justify why they were OK. That is when my life started gong in the wrong direction.

I did not honor my mother and father. I did not respect authority. I did not treat my body right; I started to smoke, have sex, and drink. I did not tithe or give money to my church. I did not respect women, their beauty, or their bodies. I did not attend church, pray, or study my Bible. I lied to people to get what I wanted. I could go on. If your life is headed in the wrong direction, it is because your principles are off. The principles you live by have come from your own head, movies, or the music to which you listen. I encourage you to find the principles God wants you to live by and watch your life do a 180.

I will share the three principles I started living by when I began my 180 voyage back in 2009.

1. *Attend church every Sunday.* I was not attending a local church, and I knew a 180 was not possible without that attendance. I knew this because I needed a community that was trying to obtain the same thing I was; that was change. So, I jumped in headfirst, and I promise you it was one of the best decisions I ever made. I have found my gifts, purpose, and life calling. I met my wife, best friends,

and mentors in the church. This one change has impacted my life in so many ways.

2. *Read a chapter from my Bible every day. I knew I needed to change my habits; but, honestly, I did not want to change everything. There were some principles in my life that I knew I would struggle with. I made up my mind to do whatever God instructed me to do according to the Bible. This gave me great direction on what new principles I should add to this list. The book of Proverbs is a great place to start.*

3. *I would forgive others. When I grasped the idea that God forgave me of all my mistakes through Jesus, I knew I had to forgive others. That included forgiving my father, people who hurt me, and, most importantly, myself for all of the pain I caused others. This was huge for me. I could not move on because I was holding myself prisoner to my own mistakes.*

How I feel is not important. My feelings cannot shake my principles. Other people's opinions cannot shake them either. When others, or your feelings, can talk you out of your principles, then you have to go back and recheck your values and priorities. The principles you live by build or destroy your character and identity. Eric Thomas said, "Behind every principle is a promise."3 The 180 happens when you apply the principle consistently and not according to how you feel.

Now, it is your turn. List three new principles you will begin living by today:

1. _____

2 _____

3. _____

◆ RETHINK YOUR PURPOSE

One of my favorite lines when sharing my faith is: "You are not here just to eat, drink, sleep, make money, have fun, and die." You are here for a purpose. Can you answer this question correctly: "Why are you here (on earth and living)?" Many people do not have an answer to this question or they have the wrong answer. You cannot create your own purpose. People who try to create their own purpose end up climbing a ladder and getting to the very top, only to realize the ladder is leaning on the wrong building.

For someone to find his or her purpose the person must go to the Creator to find it. I am speaking of the Trinity: God the Father, God the Son, and God the Holy Spirit. I found my purpose, teaching, and leading to change lives by surrendering myself to God, my pastor and by following those three principles I shared earlier. So, why are you here? By doing a 180 you will eventually run into your purpose.

What do you think your purpose is? Why do you think this is your purpose?

_____

_____

_____

_____

_____

_____

_____

_____

◆ RETHINK YOUR RELATIONSHIPS

I am going to make this simple because we tend to think too deeply about this subject. Remember all your values, priorities, and principles? If you follow them your relationships will automatically fall in line. As Amos 3:3 says, "Can two walk together, unless they are agreed?" So, when you stay true to your priorities and values, people who are not supporting you in those things will weed themselves out of your life. Let's be honest: there are people in your life who hinder you from making the positive changes you are trying to make.

I remember when I used to smoke marijuana, and I fell in love with smoking. I also hung out with people who smoked marijuana. I later decided to value my mental, emotional, and physical health. Therefore, I start prioritizing reading and playing basketball instead of smoking. I began to live by the principle of not smoking, because smoking was destroying me, and I wanted life and life more abundantly (John 10:10). When I made that decision for my life, the people with whom I hung out were OK with it—for about two weeks. After two weeks my so-called friends began pressuring me to smoke and told me I was tripping. I was angry, and I never went back to the location where they smoked.

Guess what? I stopped receiving phone calls from those people, and they stopped asking me to hang out. Why? Because my values, priorities, and principles became different. Your relationships depend on the principles you live out every day. When you change your principles, you change your relationships.

Sadly, many people who need a 180 in their lives do not want to separate from the friends who are holding them back, because they have known these friends since the third grade or they have done some great things for them. I plead with you: rethink the relationships you have with others. Some people just must leave your life. You do not have to tell your friends to go kick rocks and have that tough conversation with them. Just live by your values, priorities, and principles every day.

Ask your friends to join you in doing the new things you are doing. Remain faithful in rejecting those things that you do not value and watch how your relationships change. The right people will come into your life.

Answer the following questions:

What things that go against your new values will you say no to when your friends ask you to do them?

_____

_____

_____

_____

_____

_____

List some activities that are in line with your values to which you will invite your friends.

_____

_____

_____

_____

_____

_____

I must add, you do not have to invite your friends to everything. Just choose a couple of things as the opportunity arises. Let them know you are making some changes in your life; they may be supportive and encourage you. They may start changing themselves. Your friends' 180s could be in line with your 180. Or, your friends may try to hinder you or leave you alone altogether. It is OK if that happens. Remember, your entire life, or important areas of your life, has been going in the wrong direction. It is up to you to make the necessary adjustments to turn your own life around.

When you have made your 180, and you have been constantly living your new life, go back and try to help your friends, if they will receive it. Know, however, that you cannot help the people you love if you are not strong enough to help them. I will never forget the time I tried to help my friends stop smoking. It was a great effort, but I was too weak to help them out. After three days I was right back to smoking with them. I had to leave that environment completely to get strong enough to end my habit After I gained my strength and quit smoking for a substantial amount of time, I could go back helping others to quit smoking.

◆ RETHINK YOUR END (DEATH)

Sometimes thinking about your death is a hard thing to do. Even though it can be hard, it is beneficial. You must realize that we are all dying. Just as you have a birthday, you also have a death day. So take a moment and ponder the thought, "It's only when we realize we are terminal that we start treating time with the respect it desreves."[4] We shouldn't be afraid of death; we should respect it and use it for motivation to become all God has created us to become in the short time we have on this earth. When we think about death and are not afraid of that day, then we can truly live to our fullest potential.

Here are some questions to consider as you rethink your end:

- What legacy do I want to leave my family, friends, and the world?
- How do I want to be remembered?
- Where will I go after I die? Am I sure of my eternal destination?
- Will I have regrets when I die? Would I approve of what those closest to me will say about me after I am gone?
- Are other people better because I lived?

A lot of people say, "Only God can judge me." The question is, what will He judge? You have to get real about your own death if you are going to do a 180.

Your death is not about you. Your death is about the people whom you will precede in death. It's about all the decisions you made and how those decisions blessed other people. My grandparents will live forever because of the decisions they made and the impact they made on my life and others. What about you? Do you have regrets about your bad decisions? Do you regret not valuing God or your family? Not having nonnegotiables? My friend, it is time to do a 180.

As this chapter comes to an end, please write the many things you want to accomplish before you die. What do you want your loved ones to say about you? What impact do you want to leave on the world?

RENOUNCE

In chapter 1 we rethought some key areas of our lives. Now it is time to renounce people, things, spirits, and anything else that is stopping us from doing a 180. According to the Merriam-Webster dictionary, the word *renounce* means "to give up, refuse, or resign usually by formal declaration." It also means "to refuse to follow, obey, or recognize any further."[1] That is what we are going to do in this chapter. We are going to renounce anything that is keeping us from doing a 180. Discovering that you have the power to renounce what is holding you back is empowering!

I think all of our lives are full of things that need to be renounced. We must be careful to not allow things into our lives that we really do not want there. Renouncing those things you do not desire in your life is a constant process. Once you know the principles you want to live by, you have to renounce the things that try to get you to do the opposite.

Unfortunately, you cannot make up your mind to do something and not face any opposition. This is war—and the moment you decide to do a 180 it will seem as if everyone and everything is trying to stop you. Every time I attempt to make a change for the better, some form of opposition pops up. I think one of the biggest oppositions is fear.

As humans, we tend to dislike and fear change. Most of us only change when we absolutely have to, or are forced to. There is nothing wrong with that either. Our lives could be dramatically different if we were not fearful of change and did so without being forced. Is the grass greener on the other side? It is, especially if you need a 180 in your life. Embrace change, embrace the new, and renounce the old life you have been living.

In his book *"The Last Arrow,"* Pastor Erwin McManus wrote about fear. "When we run in fear, we're only postponing the inevitable. We will eventually have to face those fears. We will eventually have to fight those battles. Running only makes us weaker and makes our opposition stronger."[2] We must overcome our fear of change, or those things we really want to renounce will only become stronger.

Overcoming fear is not the easiest thing in the

world to do. If it were that easy everyone would be walking around fearless and bold. This is why it is so important to not fear death, because if you do not fear death then speaking a hard truth will seem easier. The only way to overcome fear is to love. The apostle John said, "There is no fear in love; but perfect love casts out fear, because fear involves torment. But he who fears has not been made perfect in love" (1 John 4:18). You have to love God, yourself, and other people—enough to make fear disappear. Do not allow the fear of rejection, failure, and change stop you from achieving your 180.

◆ **YOU MUST RENOUNCE YOUR SIN**

You may love it. You may be addicted to it. You may enjoy it. But your sin has to go! Getting rid of sin is one of those nonnegotiables. I guarantee you that you need a 180 in your life because of sin. Sin causes misdirection and confusion. What is sin? Just in case you do not know, let me explain. *Sin* means to miss the mark. Specifically, sin means to miss God's standard for our lives. It is the refusal to do what God has commanded. Do you have a good relationship with sin? Are you OK with disobeying God? It is time, once again, to be honest. Write down all the sinful thoughts and behaviors in which you are currently participating.

_____

_____

_____

_____

If by any chance you do not fill up all four lines, please ask God to open your eyes to your sinful ways and habits. Trust me, the closer you are to God, the more He reveals your sin.

The thoughts and behaviors you just listed are destroying your life and are the very causes of you going in the wrong direction. Sin is sneaky as well because it can take years for the consequences to reveal themselves. That is why you must renounce your sin immediately.

The only one, real way to get rid of sin is through Jesus Christ, the Son of the living God. He is the cure for sin. That is why He came. Jesus came to get rid of sin and give you the power to renounce it. Without Him, you will always struggle with your sin, and you will remain powerless over it. Without Jesus, your sin will continue to dominate and control you. Without Him, there is no way you can do a 180, no matter how hard you try. In my first book *Unmasked*, I gave practical principles to overcome specific sins. The entire book is the story of how I did a 180 and renounced the sin in my life.

My heart grieves because we live in a culture where sin is openly acceptable. Sin is destroying families, our children, and our entire world as we know it. As we close this section let us take a look at this accurate depiction of sin from A. W. Tozer:

> Sin, I repeat, in addition to anything else it may be, is always an act of wrong judgment. To commit a sin a man must for the moment believe that things are different from what they really are; he must confound values; he must see the moral universe out of focus; he must accept a lie as truth and see truth as a lie; he must ignore the signs on the highway and drive with his eyes shut; he must act as if he had no soul and was not accountable for his moral choices.
>
> Sin is never a thing to be proud of. No act is wise that ignores remote consequences, and sin always does. Sin sees only today, or at most tomorrow; never the day after tomorrow; next month or next year. Death and judgment are pushed aside as if they did not exist and the sinner becomes for the time a practical atheist who by his act denies not only the existence of God but the concept of life after death.[3]

Seriously, renounce your sin!

◆ RENOUNCE YOUR BAD HABITS

All of us have bad habits. Just because you have renounced your sin, it does not mean you have overcome all the bad habits you have created along the way. Once you reject your sin and begin to move on, your bad habits will begin to cry out to you. They will begin to talk to you and yell at you. Your bad habits will remind you of how good they felt and all the good times you had. They will begin to urge you and pull on you as never before. Your bad habits will make you feel guilty and powerless. So, you may be asking, "How in the world do I renounce my bad habits?" That is a great question.

First of all, you must know about your bad habits. Some people do not think smoking is a bad habit. Some people do not think lying is a bad habit. Some people do not think being disrespectful to others is a bad habit. Some people do not think eating pizza and a tub of ice cream every day for dinner is a bad habit. But, if you are going to change your bad habits, you have to agree that they are indeed bad habits! You have to be honest. Some people have trouble with being honest with themselves. Ask your five closest family members and friends what are your bad habits. They will tell you with no hesitation. Now, if you are still having trouble identifying your bad habits, download the John Maxwell Leadership Podcast, and listen to episodes 3–6, the episodes about blind spots.[4]

Write down all of your bad habits.

_____

_____

_____

_____

_____

_____

_____

Getting rid of the bad habits you listed is very simple; you replace bad habits with good habits. Reading, exercise, praying for your family, writing, calling family members to encourage them, working on your dream, and so much more are good habits to form. As you establish good habits, the bad habits will suddenly disappear. But you cannot do this alone. You need some accountability. You need to tell someone the good habits you are trying to form and then give that person permission to constantly push you to do them.

One of my personal values is being healthy. Therefore, one of my priorities is exercise. That is nice to say on paper; but in real life, I did not exercise. I have a horrible habit of not going to the gym,. I enjoy playing basketball, which is a form of exercise. Plus, I get to minister to others. Again, I have a habit of skipping basketball sessions for no reason but laziness. So, one day while getting dressed, I realized my pants barely fit. I had gained fifteen pounds, and the pounds seemed to go right to my waist. I immediately had to form a new habit around exercise. I needed a 180 in this area, or else I could be in a lot of trouble at a young age

I listen to the Sleepless Knights podcast hosted by David Shands. David talks about people not forming good habits because of the lack of immediate consequences.[5] I thought he was so right. My weight gain was not an immediate consequence; therefore, I kept my bad habits. So David uses a method with himself and others. He simply bets people. You will have to listen to the podcast for more details. I will share with you the bet I made as it relates to exercise.

My friend Josh was telling me how he needed to work out more. Here is how our texting conversation went.

Me (Mo):
Let's Bet!!!!

Josh:
Lol huh?

So, we must go to the gym 3 times a week. If I don't, I owe you $10. If you don't, you owe me $10. If we both don't, we must give $10 to someone who needs it. If we both do, we good.

Okay, I like that! How are we going to hold each other accountable, and we should start next week lol so I can clear some time.

Either we agree on times and days together or we text each other when we leave the gym...

Okay, cool.

Guess what? My habit of going to the gym is form-ing and becoming stronger because I have someone holding me accountable. I created an immediate consequence for myself so I can feel the pain of not working out right away. I had to give Josh ten dollars the other day because I only went to the gym twice last week. Giving him that money hurt. Lord knows, I do not want to experience that pain again. I would rather experience the pain of doing what I am sup-posed to do, not the consequences of my inaction. I do not know what you need to do to be held accountable, but I encourage you to find a way to form new habits. No excuses, because your life or areas of your life need a 180.

◆ RENOUNCE NEGATIVE INFLUENCES

Negative influences are easily in the top three things I see in people who want to do a 180 but "cannot." The negative influences in your life do not just boil down your friends. These influences can be your family, that awful reality television show you con-sume every day or every week, and anything else you listen to. Sin and death entered this world because of the negative influence of Satan. Adam and Eve did not renounce their negative influence. What about you? Can you cut loose from those who influence you negatively?

I believe one of the main reasons Eve gave in to Satan is because of what Satan promised. Genesis 3:4–5 tells us: "Then the serpent said to the woman, 'You will not surely die. For God knows that in the day you eat of it your eyes will be opened, and you will be like God, knowing good and evil.'" Eve listened to the wrong voice. She listened to negative influencer and what he promised. She believed that listening to the negative influence would benefit her. She did not believe in the real consequence. She did not see her life and her family's lives going in the wrong direction. She did not hold fast to the principles she had been following.

Adam was not off the hook either. Adam heard directly from God, and he allowed Satan's influence on Eve to influence him as well. Adam listened to the wrong voice. Men, do not get me wrong: it is OK for you to listen to your wife. But if your wife should begin to talk about something contrary to what God says (God's principles), then you must hold fast to your principles, based on God's Word. I am not mad at Adam or Eve, for I would have done the same thing, and I actually have. I am guessing you have too.

We can apply three simple steps to renounce negative influences. First, be sure about your principles. If you somehow skipped all the work in chapter 1, please stop reading here and go through the first chapter. Do the work there, because if you do not know what your principles are, then you cannot work further from here. So, know your principles and be unwilling to compromise on your nonnegotiables, no matter how it feels or what somebody has promised you. Remember you have to *do* this.

Second, say no! The word *no* is a complete sentence all by itself. When a negative influencer says something to you, say no. You do not owe anyone an explanation. Most of the time you know if what someone is asking you to do is wrong; but you want to be nice, loved, and accepted, so you say yes. *Your life is going in the wrong direction. Say no!*

Third, accept responsibility for the past and keep moving forward. Adam and Eve blamed others for their bad life choices. Your 180 will happen only if you take responsibility and do not even blame the negative influencer. If you are going to point a finger at someone, point it at yourself because you did not stay true to your principles, fulfill your priorities, and value your values. You must own your past mistakes, and their consequences, and keep your 180 moving. Accepting personal responsibility for your actions sets you free and gives you control. When you blame others, change is in the hands of the persons you blamed. When you accept personal responsibility, you take control over the situation and now have the power to transform.

◆ RENOUNCE THE PAST

For this entire year our church theme verses have been: "Not that I have already attained, or am already perfected; but I press on, that I may lay hold of that for which Christ Jesus has also laid hold of me. Brethren, I do not count myself to have apprehended; *but one thing I do, forgetting those things which are behind* and reaching forward to those things which are ahead, I press toward the goal for the prize of the upward call of God in Christ Jesus" (Phil. 3:12–13, emphasis added). Did you pick up on what the writer, the apostle Paul, said? He is essentially saying to us, "I have room to improve, and the one thing I do above all others is to forget those things that are behind." The only way we are going to do a 180 is if we forget our past and move on.

Unfortunately, God has blessed us with a memory. Memory is a God-given gift, and it should be used to help us, not tear us down. I believe a lot of our memories are hindering us from the future. Think about it. You remember all of your failures and successes. You remember all the pain and hurt you went through. You remember all the good times with your good friends. Doing a 180 causes you to intentionally go in the opposite direction. When you go in that direction, oftentimes you cannot carry your past with you.

There is a powerful account in Genesis chapter 19 where a family was directed to do a 180. God was getting ready to destroy everything in their past. Before I continue with this story, I cannot help but point out that God wants to destroy everything in your past as if it never happened. God wants us to move from our past so when He destroys it we are not there! Life is meant to be lived, not relived. But back to the story. Just before God destroyed the city that represented the past for Lot and his family, He gave them specific instructions. Please take careful note of God's instructions.

God told Lot and his family (1) to escape for their lives; (2) to not look back; and (3) where to escape. If they did not escape they would be swept away. I feel God, in this very moment, is telling you the same thing. You have some areas in your life that are about to destroy you and your family. God is telling you to escape for your lives. You may have pornography or a shopping addiction. You may be in an abusive relationship. You may be lazy, unmotivated, lost, brokenhearted, confused about life, or just tired of everyday trials. You need to escape for your life and *do not look back*. Renounce your past. God has already told you where to escape. That may be a church, it may be the police, or it may be a different city or environment. All you know is you have to escape for your life.

Now, Lot's wife was from Sodom and Gomorrah. She had friendships and memories there. So, as the city was being destroyed, she looked back. At the moment she looked back she became a pillar of salt and was hindered from moving into the future—literally. Please learn from this story. If you are going to do a real 180 in any aspect of your life, then you need to renounce your past. Do not look back; looking back hinders forward progress. Forget those things that are behind you and press on.

REDIRECT

I have a brother with whom I am very close. We are one year and eleven days apart in age. So we grew up tightly knit; and, of course, we always competed against each other. We both love the game of basketball and were first called "Brooks brothers" on the court. My brother writes with his right hand and shoots with his left. I write with my left hand and shoot with my right. We played a lot of one-on-one growing up, and I happened to be a phenomenal defensive player. Yeah, I said it—phenomenal.

Every time my brother would go for a left-hand layup, I would block his shot. I kid you not, I blocked his left-hand layup hundreds of times. Then something amazing happened; he adjusted. Once he adjusted, I did too and still got some good blocks on him. I have to admit, he adjusted and redirected so much that, eventually, I could no longer block his shot. He learned how to use his body and adjust midair. I had no idea what he was going to do next. In the same way my brother adjusted his layups to prevent me from blocking his shots, you have to adjust in order to change any aspect of your life. Redirecting your life is all about making the necessary adjustments to change your life.

Adjustments are not like a light switch you turn on and off at will. They take commitment and diligence. My pastor defines diligence as being maximum effort over a sustained period of time. You have to give these adjustments everything you have or they will not work. Even if you fail, do not give up. Keep adjusting, keep being self-aware, and keep your commitment. I want to provide one more real-life example of how I made adjustments in my life.

Unfortunately, I am an ex-smoker. I remember several occasions when I tried to kick the habit. For goodness' sake, I have asthma; so I began to rethink this whole smoking habit. Was it worth the risk of yellow teeth, yellow eyes, shortness of breath, failed drug tests, and eventual cancer? The answer was easy: of course not! Then I began to renounce the habit. I told myself and my friends that I had quit smoking. Well, guess how long that lasted? Sometimes a day, or three days; I may have gone a week without smoking. I was puzzled at my lack of results. I really wanted to quit smoking, so why was it difficult to stop?

I was having difficulty quitting smoking because I was not being true to what I said I valued—my health. More importantly, I needed to redirect and adjust key areas in my life in order to do a 180. I had to replace the habit of smoking with something else. Just renouncing it was not enough; I had to fill the void left by not smoking. That is what redirect is all about. Redirect is about replacing your old habits with new habits that will help you sustain your values.

This chapter may be the glue to the entire book. You can rethink and renounce, but if you do not redirect some things in your life, everything else does not matter.

◆ REDIRECT YOUR TIME

How are you spending your time, and with whom are you spending your time? Many people say time is the most valuable resource given to human beings because once it is spent it is gone. Everyone has the same twenty-four hours a day, and how you spend those twenty-four hours will determine everything about your life. I like to look at time as if it were a sponge. If you dip a sponge in milk and squeeze the sponge, milk will come out. Dip that sponge in oil and squeeze it, oil will come out. What are you dipping your time in? Please, do not expect fruitful production to take place when you are spending all your time engaging in fruitless procrastination activities.

Your life needs to change, and the only way that is going to happen is if you redirect your time. If you applied chapter 1, this should have automatically happened. Think about it: when your values, priorities, and principles change, how you spend your time changes as well. Chapter 2 was all about renouncing certain things in your life that were hindering you. The way you renounce is to spend less time with the things that are interfering with your life. So, what are your major time wasters? I believe most people see the same time wasters as broken off into three areas: media time wasters, useless activity time wasters, and social time wasters.

If you are scrolling on social media, watching hours of television, and playing video games all the time, you are literally wasting your time and life. I used to be a heavy video game player and ESPN fanatic. Then one day it dawned upon me, "Am I growing closer to God doing this? Am I making more money doing this? Am I getting closer to my dreams doing this?" The answer was a big fat no. So, if you want to really change your life, do the following.

First of all, do not go on social media for thirty straight days. Doing this one thing has blessed me in so many ways. After the thirty days I went back on social media and I felt that I had not missed a single thing. The same people were posting the same information. All the viral things that were happening all over the world that I did not know about, people would share those things with me in person. Since I did not know what was going on, others had to fill me in. My relationships with others were strengthened. After the thirty-day trial, uninstall all of your social media apps on your phone. This will help you to become intentional about going onto your social media account. If you truly want a 180, you must put in the work and make some sacrifices. Maybe that is too much for you to do right now. Turn off your notifications and move all of your apps from the front page of your phone.

◆ REDIRECT YOUR CALENDAR

Let me say this right out of the gate. If you do not have a calendar, then you are not serious about reaching your goals or changing your life. If you do not have a calendar, that means you do not have enough to do. It means you are loosey-goosey with your most valuable asset—time. In his book *Getting Things Done* author David Allen talks about getting things off your mind and into your system.[1] Yes, either you have a lot to accomplish or you need more to do; but you will never find that out if you do not have a calendar. Have you ever gotten paid and had no idea where your money went? If so, that is because you did not have a budget.

People with budgets know where every penny is spent. Your calendar helps you budget your time correctly so you can stay true to your values and priorities.

Now, let's go to work. Whatever day of the week it is today, plan the next day. Write down everything you must do or want to do tomorrow.

_____

_____

_____

_____

_____

_____

_____

At what time are you going to do those things? Please put them on your calendar.

If you find yourself unable to fit everything you listed onto your calendar, then you have to adjust something. What time do you go to sleep? What time do you wake up? When do you make time for God's Word and prayer? When are you going to work on that goal you set for yourself? These are questions that need to be answered before your day and week get started.

Redirecting your time will be the number one factor in the next half of this chapter. When you have a good grip on your time, then you can give your most precious minutes to what really matters. My 180 would never have happened without my faith, obedience, and the daily decisions I made. My life is forever changed for the better because I redirected these areas of my life.

◆ REDIRECT YOUR FAITH

When my life was going in the wrong direction, I had to take a deep look at who and what my faith is in. This was challenging, because I would always say my faith was in God. Then I finally read the words of Jesus from Matthew 15:18:

> "These people draw near to Me with their mouth,
> And honor Me with their lips,
> But their heart is far from Me."

Those words described my faith perfectly, and it was hard for me to own up to it. My lips said I trusted God and loved Him. My lips said my faith is in God and

God alone; but, honestly, my heart was so far from Him. I had faith in myself, money, friends, and a whole bunch of other stuff until I redirected my faith. This is a challenging thing to do because you must come to the realization that your faith is not as strong and as deep as you say it is. To this day I am constantly working on this.

Romans 10:17 says that "faith comes by hearing, and hearing by the word of God. How much of God are you listening to? Are you connected to a local church and learning from a Bible-teaching pastor? As instructed in James 1:22, are you being a doer of the word and not a hearer only, deceiving yourself? Are you reading your Bible daily and asking questions about various scriptures? Are you spending time in private prayer and meditation? Are you spending time praying with other believers in the body of Christ? Are you sharing your faith with other people? Are you specifically loving and forgiving other people? These are the basics of the faith; and if you are not doing these constantly, then your faith needs major redirection.

There is only one real way to redirect your faith and that is to redirect your obedience and your daily decisions. The remainder of this chapter will focus on those two things. This is where the real work begins. Faith is believing in who God said He is and doing what God said, just because He said it. Faith is trusting that

Jesus is Lord and giving your entire life to Him. Write down what you need to do to redirect your faith:

_____

_____

_____

_____

_____

◆ REDIRECT YOUR OBEDIENCE

The season was the fall of 2007, and I had just graduated high school that spring. I wanted to go to Ferris State University; but for various reasons, I did not. I had a good friend who went to Central Michigan University and a couple of friends who went to Ferris State. There was going to be a stoplight party at Ferris State, and it was supposed to be epic. You were supposed to wear red if you were taken, green if you were single, and yellow if it was complicated. I thought it was cool to wear a green, yellow, and red shirt—so I did.

As I was getting ready for the party, my mom somehow found out that I was planning to drive three hours to go to this event. At first she was OK with it.

On Thursday she asked to talk with me. She shared with me that she had a bad feeling about my going to this party and that I should not drive up there. I was so upset and angry because I wanted to go. I also did not want to listen to my mom. After all, I was eighteen years old, and I could do whatever I wanted to do. I was grown! I promise you; I actually sat and thought about that conversation all day. But, in the end, I decided to go to the party.

I made the three-hour drive from Kalamazoo, Michigan up to Ferris State University. I also made a pit stop to see my friend at Central Michigan. We partied and had a fun time. We ended the night around 3 a.m. Someone was kind enough to allow my friends and me to spend the night in their dorms. As we drove on the Ferris State campus, I felt my head nod, and I swerved a little bit. The next thing I knew there were flashing lights in my rearview mirror. I knew this good night was about to turn sour.

As we were waiting for the police to walk to the car, I begged my friends to trade seats with me because I did not have my driver's license. All of them said no and didn't seem to care about the trouble I was about to be in. They wanted to make sure they did not get into trouble, and I totally understand that. I was not mad at them at all. The officer approached the car, and I was completely honest with him. He wrote me a ticket and allowed one of my friends with a driver's license to take over the driving. As he gave me the ticket he told me I had to appear in court on Monday in Big Rapids. This was a huge problem.

My mom asked me how everything had gone on my trip. I lied and said it went well. On Monday I left Kalamazoo at 6 a.m. to get to Big Rapids for my court appointment. It was my first time in court, and I was terrified. The judge was very merciful and told me I had to pay four hundred dollars by 4 p.m. or I would have a warrant out for my arrest for the unpaid ticket. I did not have the money to pay the ticket, but I did not say anything to the judge. So I hurried back to Kalamazoo to work out a plan I had cooked up in my head.

I had my first credit card, and it had a thousand dollars on it. I knew that I was not responsible enough to have it on me, so I had allowed "you know who" to hold for me. You guessed right—my mother. I said, "Mom, I need my credit card." She quickly responded, "Why do you need it? You are not getting it unless you give me a good reason why." I could not tell her the truth. I was too prideful, afraid, and guilty. So, 4 p.m. came and went, and I had a warrant for my arrest, but nothing happened! The police did not come looking for me, and life went on as normal.

◆ EVERYTHING COMES FULL CIRCLE

In October of that same year I was driving in the car with one of my best friends and his friend. We had just finished smoking a blunt (marijuana). My blinker was broken; Lord knows, that is another story in itself. My music was loud, and good vibes were all around. Suddenly, I saw those same lights flashing in my rear-view mirror. Instantly my heart began to beat fast, and my palms began to sweat. I told my two friends that I was going to jail. They did not believe me.

When the police officer ran my name, it was evident that I had a warrant, because three more police cars arrived on the scene. They asked me to get out of my vehicle, and they put handcuffs on me. I was so embarrassed; I was pulled over on a popular street in front of the city commissioner's house. I think she called my mom to break the news. I am thankful that my mother bailed me out and I did not have to go to Big Rapids to see the judge again. I just had to pay for that ticket.

My mother, who knows more than me and has more experience than me and loves me more than any other person on this planet, had given me a command. That command was this: do not drive to Ferris State to attend that party. I had no clue that my disobedience would lead to so many unforeseen consequences. So much wasted time, money, and pain came from one decision.

Here is my entire point: your life is headed in the wrong direction because of your sin and disobedience to God. My mother is just an example of how we treat God. He gives us directions; and when we choose to do otherwise, our lives spiral out of control. The sweet thing about God is, when your life is in need of a 180, you can call on Him and He will give you more instructions to help you.

◆ REDIRECT YOUR DECISIONS

The real deal is this: Your need for a 180 is in the decisions you make. Small decisions lead to huge results! Even as I write this book, I am making small decisions that turn into great outcomes.

I will never forget one of the smallest and most impactful decisions I have ever made—a choice that has changed my life forever. The decision to stop smoking marijuana has had a ripple effect on my life that is hard to explain. My body (particularly my face and lips) changed, my mind changed, my emotions changed, my relationships changed, my conversations changed, and my spirituality changed!

At this point you should be seeing some changes already taking place because you made some decisions earlier in the book. Stop looking for the "big" decision. When you make the small decisions daily, it will create the big decision and opportunities you were not expecting. These small, daily decisions will create unbreakable habits. As we end this chapter, I want to give you two practical tips that will help you make great decisions.

DECIDE BEFORE

Life is so much easier when you make decisions before you *have* to make them. This is very similar to your nonnegotiables, from earlier in the book. Some of the best choices are the decisions you make before you are in a certain situation. You are more likely to make the wrong decision when you decide quickly in the heat of the moment. When your mind is made up beforehand, you don't feel the pressure of making on-the-spot, life-changing decisions.

When I said my vows to my wife on Saturday, June 25, 2016, I decided that day I would be faithful to her, love her unconditionally, and be with her through thick and thin. If another woman tries to entice me to cheat on my wife, guess what? I don't have to decide in the moment because I already decided beforehand. My decision was made on our wedding day. A lot of decisions should be made in advance.

WISE COUNSEL

"Blessed is the man who walks not in the counsel of the ungodly" (Psalm 1:1). That means blessed is the man who *does* walk in the counsel of the godly. When you need help deciding, it is important that you listen to the right counsel or advice. You make good decisions by surrounding yourself with others who make good decisions and have good character.

Listening to the right people will help you navigate your toughest life decisions. Remember, you are changing your life. The people to whom you listen can make or break your 180. Please be careful where you place your attention.

REHEARSE

My favorite athlete of all time is the late great, Kobe Bryant. I became a Kobe fan when I was in the second grade, while watching the 1997 NBA slam dunk contest. Kobe had a bald head, and so did I. On Kobe's final dunk, he did the between-the-legs dunk and won the contest. I wrote his name down, and I declared that he was going to be my favorite player. Wow, was that ever a good choice, because he is the basketball G.O.A.T (Greatest of All Time) in my book. So, of course, I wanted to play the game of basketball like Kobe Bryant.

I went to the playground and tried to dunk during gym class the way Kobe Bryant had, and guess what? I couldn't. Even after years of playing basketball, I never became as good as Kobe. Why? I didn't practice as Kobe practiced. In his book, *The Mamba Mentality*,

Kobe Bryant documents his on and off the court habits.[1] My mind was blown away by his hidden dedication and repetition. Of course, I had the potential to be as good as Kobe, but I did not rehearse as he did. I did not work as hard as he worked. I did not get up and hit the gym as he did. I did not watch thousands of hours of basketball film as he did. So I would be insane to think that I would be as good as Kobe Bryant without putting in the same amount of work.

Your 180 is not going to happen without rehearsing what you learned in the first three chapters of this book. Some of you will make that 180 turn and do great for three months; then if something tragic happens, you will *revert* instead of *rehearse*. You have to keep rehearsing the things that are having a great impact on your life. *Don't stop!*

One day, Kobe Bryant met with a college women basketball player. This player's team had just lost in the NCAA women's final. Kobe asked the young lady, "Did you watch the game?" The young woman asked, "Are you crazy, I cannot watch that, it is too painful." Kobe then responded, "I watch film after every loss including during the finals, you should too."[2] Kobe's point was nothing should stop you from rehearsing, even a defeat.

Here is where the hard part really kicks in. Can you rehearse when things don't go your way? Can you rehearse after failure? Can you rehearse when tragedy hits your life? Can you rehearse when you do not feel like it? When these things happen, many people revert back to what they used to do or grew up doing. This chapter is all about how to rehearse when life circumstances tell you not to rehearse—when you do not feel like rehearsing the good habits you committed to keeping or feel that following your principles at the moment is not worth the trouble. Can you rehearse anyway?

◆ REHEARSE YOUR ACCOUNTABILITY

Ecclesiastes 4:9–12 says:

> Two are better than one,
> Because they have a good reward for their labor.
> For if they fall, one will lift up his companion.
> But woe to him who is alone when he falls,
> For he has no one to help him up.

Your 180 will not and cannot be done on your own. Serious accountability will be required. *Accountability* is when another person knows where you currently are, where you are trying to go, and helps you get there. You do not need a thousand people to hold you accountable. You do need at least one other person who loves you and is serious about helping you make this 180. Yes, your accountability partner must love you, and you must have some type of relationship with that person. Trust is key as well. Without it you will not maximize this key relationship. Checking in with him or her on a regular basis is how you rehearse your accountability. Let's dive a little deeper.

KNOWS WHERE YOU ARE

Your accountability partner must know where you currently are in your 180. He or she should know what you struggle with the most. The person should know the ugly truth about where you are in your journey. Do you see why I said you need a relationship with him or her? Hiding things from your accountability partner will not benefit you. This person cannot hold you accountable for things that he or she does not know.

KNOWS WHERE YOU ARE GOING

You must clearly articulate to your accountability partner where you are going. He or she needs to know your goals and the specific things you want to change in your life. Doing a 180 doesn't mean a hill of beans if you have no sense of where you are going, who you are becoming, and the changes you desire to make.

HELPS YOU GET THERE

Getting to where you are going is the hard part. The question is, are you going to listen to the advice, lecture, and wisdom of your accountability partner? You must be able to receive constant correction, encouragement, and hard truths from this person. I have discovered that a lot of people have great loved ones who are willing to help them obtain the 180 they desire. Those same people get angry and hold grudges against those who tell them the wonderfully hard truth. *Don't do that!*

In an interview with Kristine Leahy of *Fair Game*, Caron Butler shared a story about how his former teammate Kobe Bryant held him accountable. Kobe told Caron that Mountain Dew was not good for him and would hurt him in the long run. So Butler ditched one of his bad habits because he was willing to accept a hard truth.[3]

The Mountain Dew example may seem small, but it is not. There are a lot of individuals who would have received this great advice and said, "I am grown. You can't tell me what to drink." You must possess the ability to receive the hard truth, advice, and wisdom of others. A lack of accountability will lead to the lack of growth and change you need.

◆ REHEARSE YOUR VISION

By nature, I am a dreamer. As a matter a fact my number one strength according to theCliffton Strength Finders test is, Futuristic. I cannot stop thinking about and talking about my vision. The book you are reading now is a part of my vision that has been rehearsed over and over and over again. Even when my life was a living hell, and it seemed that all hope was lost, I had a vision that if I could turn my life around I would write books, inspire people, and eventually change the world.

What vision has God put into your heart? This is an important question, because if God did not put the vision in your heart, then you will be, as the old saying goes, climbing up a ladder, getting to the top, and realizing that you are leaning on the wrong building. Before you start climbing make sure you are on the right building. Now, back to the question at hand: What vision has God put into your heart?

Please know that if God gave you a vision, then it always ends with you being a blessing to someone else. What you do and accomplish leads to lives being changed by your actions. I really pray that this book is helping and blessing you. Write down what you see yourself doing in the future. How will you bless people?

_____

_____

_____

_____

_____

Rehearse that vision! Write it down; talk about it (to trusted people); read about it; and, most importantly, take action. Go after your vision with everything you have. You may fail. If you do, get up and rehearse again. You may be discouraged. Get up and rehearse again. You may be laughed at and talked about. Get up and rehearse again. You may be misunderstood. Get up and rehearse again. You may be disappointed. Get up and rehearse again. It doesn't matter what happens in your life; continue to rehearse the vision of the 180 you see. My friend, you will get there!

◆ REHEARSE YOUR PERSPECTIVE

I define _perspective_ as the way you respond to something. I can pinpoint your perspective, based on your response to what has been said or done. The way you look at and respond to all situations will determine how long your 180 will take. A negative perspective will produce movement in the wrong direction. A positive perspective will produce movement in the best direction. It is vital that you grow your positive perspective.

I truly believe that everything that occurs in life is to be used to help us get to where we are destined to be; therefore, I respond accordingly. Of course, I haven't perfected this yet, and I'd like to think I am getting closer every day. My situation does not matter; I count it all joy (James 1:2) because I know it must produce patience and work out for my good (Romans 8:28). When "negative" things happen in my life, I follow three steps.

First, I acknowledge the pain. I admit that it hurts. I don't try to pretend that whatever happened didn't happen. I take a long hard look at the honest truth. I own my feelings and the pain of that negative experience. I acknowledge the pressure I feel or even the anger that is taking place.

Second, I pray. I tell God how I feel and why I am frustrated. I ask Him to help me to respond in a way where I know somehow this is good for me. I rehearse back to God all of His promises to me. I know God knows me better than I know myself, so I am 100 percent honest with Him.

Here is a little nugget on prayer. Stop using prayer as a means to soothe your feelings. Let me show you what that looks like. You pray, then go tell others you prayed, and you are looking for brownie points

because you prayed. Jesus said we are to pray in secret, and God "who sees in secret will reward you
openly" (Matthew 6:6).

Third, I take action. I respond in such a way that
I know my situation is going to end up working for
me somehow and in some way. If a person "did me
wrong," then I forgive him or her and even take responsibility, whether or not I think I am at fault. If it
is something totally out of my control, such as death,
boss decision, or anything else, I trust the continual
process where God has placed me. My perspective
produces my results. It is all about how you see things.
You can decide how you see any situation.

◆ REHEARSE YOUR WHY

Your *why* is the last and most important thing you
should rehearse. Here is the reason: Sometimes, when
the going gets tough, we tend to forget why we are
doing what we are doing. You are making this 180
journey, and it is important that you don't forget your
why. Why are you turning your life around? Why are
you making new and different decisions? Why are
you sacrificing so much? For whom are you doing it?
Whatever that reason is, it is important not to forget
it in the midst of trying times.

Rehearsing is so important because you tend to
remember what you rehearse. You will never forget

how to ride a bike because of all the rehearsing you did. You will never forget how to tie your shoe because of all the practice you put in. This principle makes sense when I talk about elementary elements of rehearsing. When it comes to our why, we tend to forget when things are not going the way we think they should.

So, why do you want to turn your life around? For whom do you want to do it? Whenever you come across challenges, detours, closed doors, disappointments, drama, stress, and feel like giving up, think about your why and keep going. Think about who you would be letting down if you quit now. Think about who you would be disappointing if you picked that bad habit back up again. Know your why and rehearse your why.

During my 180, there were so many opportunities to go back to my old life. One thing that kept me from doing so was my why. I didn't have kids at the time; but one of my whys was my children that I hoped to have someday. As I was writing this book, our first child was born. My why also included my wife, family, the youth I lead, and Jesus. I think my biggest why was my future. I knew that if I did not do a 180, my future and potential would be in danger. Man's greatest weight is unused capacity. Lift that weight by remembering why you are making this 180 and blow the lid off your capacity.

FINAL WORDS

As this book comes to a close, I want your self-assessment to be at an all-time high. There is no way you can reach your full potential by doing the same things you are doing now. You can't reach it by hanging out with the same group of people you are hanging out with now. You can't do it without making 180s in various areas of your life.

Making a 180 can bring forth fear in you that you didn't know existed. So, in order to do a 180, you must behave like a turtle. There is only one way a turtle can move forward and make progress. The turtle must have all four legs and head outside of its shell. The only problem with that is, the turtle is most vulnerable and exposed to danger when it is outside of its exterior. So, in order for the turtle to move, it must leave the safety of its shell to move forward.

My friend, if you want to move forward with your life, and fulfill your potential, you must come out of your shell. Yes, you will expose yourself to attacks in the form of criticism, negative people, and those who don't want to make the 180. None of that matters at the finish line; everything you have experienced will be worth it. You will experience pain. Either the pain of change or the pain of staying the same. Just know you won't be able to avoid it.

Please allow me to pray for you.

> Father God, in Jesus name I want to thank You for who You are. You are good, loving, and just; and You want the best for us, Your children. Lord, I pray for the readers of this book. I pray that You will strengthen them for the work ahead. You never promised an easy life; so I ask that You would give these readers the wisdom to make sound choices. I ask that You would provide mercy, and grant them enough time to make their 180s for Your glory. Thank You for loving them, and please continue to show Yourself strong on their behalf. In Jesus name, amen.

NOTES

Chapter 1: Rethink

1. Anonymous quote.
2. Eric Thomas, *Average Skill Phenomenal Will* (n.p.: ETA Publications, 2015), 4.
3. Eric Thomas, "5 Feelings," YouTube mp3, March 31, 2014, https://youtu.be/lEAdNIg8xwU.
4. Erwin Raphael McManus, *The Last Arrow: Save Nothing for the Next Life* (New York: Waterbrook, 2017), 96.

Chapter 2: Renounce

1. *Merriam-Webster*, s.v. "renounce (*v.*),"accessed October 7, 2019, https://www.merriam-webster.com/dictionary/renounce.
2. Erwin Raphael McManus, *The Last Arrow: Save Nothing for the Next Life* (New York: Waterbrook), 122.
3. A. W. Tozer, *Man: The Dwelling Place of God*, AW Tozer Books (Book 3) (CreateSpace, 2017), 30.

4. *The John Maxwell Leadership Podcast* (2018)
5. [[Placeholder for David Shands Sleepless Knights podcast note]]

Chapter 3: Redirect

1. David Allen, *Getting Things Done: The Art of Stress-Free Productivity*, rev. ed. (New York: Penguin Books, 2015).

Chapter 4: Rehearse

1. Kobe Bryant, *The Mamba Mentality: How I Play* (New York: MCD Books, 2018).
2. Bryant, interview by Lewis Howes, September 9, 2018, YouTube video, 23:58, https://youtu.be/WY0wONSarXA
3. Caron Butler, interview by Kristine Leahy, *Fair Game*, December 26, 2018, YouTube video, 5:25, https://www.youtube.com/watch?v=JJoDZbagTLU.

Connect with Mo

Social Media

Facebook: https://www.facebook.com/mobrooks
ONE/?ref=bookmarks
Instagram: mo_brooks1
Twitter: mo_brooks
Website: www.mobrooks1.com
Podcast: The Mo Brooks "Life" Podcast
Other Books by Mo Brooks
Unmasked: The Courage to Be You

Recommended Workshop or Conference Primary Topics *(Not limited to these)*

180: What to Do when Your Life Is Headed in the Wrong Direction
Fly or Fall
Enhancing Youth Ministry
Bullying and Suicide Prevention
How to Unmask: The Courage to Be You
How to Share Christ with Others
Overcoming Bad Habits
Breaking the Cycle
Love Thyself (Building Self-Esteem)

Mo Brooks on October30, 2008 (19 years old)

Mo Brooks in the year of 2019 (30 years old)

Your 180 is possible!
Believe it!

MO BROOKS IGNITES

Made in the USA
Monee, IL
25 July 2020

36949113R00046